C000172375

CUBISM was an avant-grad
emerged in the early 20th c
by Pablo Picasso and Georç
considered one of the most influential a.
movements of the 20th century. Cubism
radically transformed the way artists
approached representation in art, departing
from traditional perspectives and introducing
new ways of seeing and depicting the world.

Key characteristics of Cubism include.
1.Geometric Shapes:
2. Multiple Perspectives
3. Fragmentation
4.Anaytical Cubism
5.Synthetic Cubism:

Prominent Cubist Artists:
- Pablo Picasso
George Braque

In the pages of this book are some images
which mimic Cubistic styled paintings. These
images are for references only and aspiring
artists are encouraged to create their own
forms, textures and coloration to make their
Cubist style painting stand out in a museum
and/or art gallery

Art No. 01

Art No. 02

Art No. 03

Art No. 05

Art No. 06

Art No. 07

Art No. 08

Art No. 09

Art No. 10

Art No. 11

Art No. 12

Art No. 13

Art No. 14

Art No. 15

Art No. 16

Art No. 17

Art No. 18

Art No. 19

Art No. 20

Art No. 21

Art No. 22

Art No. 23

Art No. 24

All images of art have been AI generated

Art Cofre

Printed in Great Britain
by Amazon